CW00540416

B
7
A

Parables

COMMUNICATING GOD ON EARTH

CWR

Christine Leonard

Front cover image: Roger Walker
Concept development, editing, design and production by CWR
Printed in the UK by Linney Group

ISBN: 978-1-85345-340-3

Contents

Introduction

'Tell me a story.' Those words have power. 'Jesus, tell me a story!', when you come to think about it, is even more extraordinary. Jesus told over 60 stories which make up one third of His recorded teaching in Matthew, Mark and Luke's Gospels. Most of the Bible is made up of, not doctrine, but stories, true or fictional.

Stories? Oh no, not childish and cosy once-upon-a-time sessions, complete with actions to jolly ditties about houses on the rock! If you've known these stories since you were tiny perhaps they seem simplistic and over-familiar – yet Jesus told none of them to children. Christians avoid singing (or, for the most part, preaching) about a few shockingly difficult parables. Why, for example, is God or His kingdom like an unjust judge? Why does Jesus commend a thoroughly dishonest manager? Childish? Easy? Cosy? Think again!

Maybe you weren't brought up in a church setting and are wondering what relevance 2,000-year-old tales of vines and shepherds, of by-gone meal etiquette and the power of petty Middle-Eastern overlords have to your life today. Consider what stories do. They can warn or give hope, perhaps encoding the truth in dangerous times. They may calm and reassure, or scare and inflame. They help us to understand our world and the way individuals, groups, factions and hierarchies 'tick' and relate. They can be moral tales, showing us how to behave. They can illustrate an argument, or engage our emotions and teach us to care. They may attract, excite, amuse and entertain us, or puzzle and even alienate us. They may show us heroes to follow or anti-heroes to shun. They may open our eyes to great beauty and goodness, or to evil and ugliness. They enlarge us – through them we travel to other worlds, other dimensions, and experience things impossible by other means. They can surprise and subvert, breaking moulds. They can change our thinking, our ways of seeing, our behaviour, even our society, by provoking us to ask questions and to 'think outside of the box'. Jesus' stories and pithy sayings, together with the stories about His life which interweave with them, do all these things and more.

The word 'parable' means more than a story. In both Old and New Testaments it means 'two things placed alongside one another for purposes of comparison'. Parables are metaphors, then, and similes, occasionally allegories and often stories that say 'this is like that'. John's Gospel has no story-parables but 'I am the vine' or 'I am the good shepherd' are, in this wider sense, parables. Jesus' saying: 'It is easier for a camel to go through the eye of a needle than for a rich man to enter the kingdom of God' (Matt. 19:24; Mark 10:25; Luke 18:25), is also a comparison, a parable. It paints a vivid picture and sets a scene which could be the start of a story. It causes puzzlement – another meaning of 'parable' is 'dark saying' or 'riddle'.

Above all, though, Jesus was the supreme storyteller – at meals, on journeys, to crowds as part of His teaching, in disputes as part of His argument. No other literature had stories like His – apart from a few parables in the Old Testament. Greeks had fables with talking animals – or well-argued philosophy. Jewish rabbinical parables abounded. Some theologians think Jesus drew on that tradition, but many rabbinical parables were written down after Jesus' time and may well have imitated Him rather than the other way round. Anyway, placed alongside Jesus' stories, most lack depth.

Jesus' parables don't expound a neat, systematic theology: they're about life, often ordinary life, seen from a very different perspective – God's. And since, as Isaiah 55:8–9 says, God's thoughts are not our thoughts, pinning down the exact meaning isn't easy. In *The Radical Stories of Jesus*, Michael Ball cites 17 different theologians, each with his own theory which led to a different (and often plausible) interpretation of one short, simple parable – the seed growing secretly. Such ambiguity could make for lively discussion as you work through these studies! But these parables aren't about philosophy or knowing something, they're about knowing and relating to someone – to God and to 'your neighbour'. That kind of knowledge involves dialogue, questioning, empathising, listening, using your imagination – above all, praying. Ask the Holy Spirit, who will 'guide you into all truth' (John 16:13), for help.

Why were parables – whether stories or picture-sayings – Jesus' chosen way of verbal communication? I've sat through complex lectures on 'How to communicate the gospel in our postmodern world'. All have boiled down to: 'Use stories, images and pithy sayings, and discussion in small groups.' Jesus knew a thing or two! We can learn much, not only from what He said, but from how He communicated with different groups of people – and that's how we'll approach these studies. At times Jesus needed to hide some of His meaning from enemies or from an over-enthusiastic crowd but explained more to close friends. At other times, like the Old Testament before Him and Shakespeare's *Hamlet* after Him, Jesus used a story to 'catch the conscience' if not of the king, then of a powerful person or group. If we're to be His mouth and arms, His ambassadors, then we need to learn how, as well as what, to communicate to different people – how to paint heaven on this earth.

WEEK 1

To hide and to reveal: parables and their uses

Opening Icebreaker and Worship

The leader produces an object covered with a cloth and asks everyone to guess what the cloth is hiding.

'Now we see but a poor reflection as in a mirror; then we shall see face to face. Now I know in part; then I shall know fully, even as I am fully known' (1 Cor. 13:12). Sing, read or listen to something which expresses the mystery of God. Worship Him for what we've yet to know of Him.

Bible Readings

- 2 Samuel 12:1–14
- Isaiah 5:1–13
- Matthew 7:28–29; 13:10–17, 34–35, 51–52
- Luke 9:44–48

Opening Our Eyes

'Evangelism,' the preacher announced, 'is like curly, overgrown toenails.' The analogy certainly drew the congregation's attention. Surprising people, hiding its meaning like a riddle, it got us thinking. The explanation? Both are things people want to cover up in the hope that they will go away.

Parables are comparisons – riddles, metaphors, illustrations or stories. Old Testament prophets used parables to bring God's truth in disguise, surprising people out of the rut of their wrong thinking. Even with a largely good king, like David, maybe it was dangerous to state an unpalatable truth head on. In 2 Samuel 12:1–14 the prophet Nathan appealed to David's best side, his desire to rule the people justly – told him his story and then turned David's fierce judgment against David himself. Echoes of our second reading appear in Jesus' stories and Paul's symbolism. Isaiah was not the first, or the last, Bible writer to compare Israel (or the Church) with viniculture. He aimed to 'catch the conscience', not of the king this time, but of the rich and powerful of his nation who neglected the poor while indulging themselves to excess. They believed their riches were a sign of God's blessing – but the prophet tells a very different story, along with a stark warning for them to mend their ways. The great theme of social justice, reflecting the righteous rule of God over His kingdom, threads through most stories of the Bible, including the parables. Perhaps that's because it requires an exercise of the imagination to break the status quo and to live differently. The people of Isaiah's day had a reminder of his warning every time they looked at a vineyard. What symbol might a prophet use today to convey the same much-needed message to some parts of the Church?

Parables carry a mixed message, hiding within riddles but also revealing truths formerly hidden. After He's told many parables, the crowds see Jesus as 'one who had authority, and not as their teachers of the law' (Matt. 7:28–29). Ever heard a preacher expound a scripture to death, over-complicating it so that your head hurts and you think – I could never do what this verse says? Jewish teachers, with their *Midrash* on every verse, their, 'Rabbi X says this, Y that, and Z the other' must have had a similar effect – but the crowd found Jesus' stories clear, authoritative and easy to understand. He used everyday examples to explain another dimension of life to them – while His actions gave a wider context to His words.

Matthew 13:34–35 expresses this 'revealing' side of parables but, just as we think 'stories help people see things', Jesus' words in Matthew 13:10–17 stress the exact opposite. Then, in just four verses (Luke 9:44–48) speaking to His disciples, Jesus conceals one thing and reveals something else. Confused? Let me pose a question-parable. You're invited, as a Christian, but within the usual constraints, to tell students and staff in a large secondary school about Christian salvation. Various problems arise. Many students, hearing your words about freedom and forgiveness, refuse to do any homework and run amok. Those who are already Christians scare off their friends with hell-fire talk. Some enemies of the gospel among the staff argue your words are prohibited by law within that context. Others, calling themselves Christians, enforce a graceless authority. If you'd told stories, might they not have revealed things to some and hidden truth from others, until they were ready to receive it?

Discussion Starters

1. 2 Samuel 12:1–14. Can you think of any other examples, not necessarily in the Bible, where a story has been used to 'catch the conscience of the king' – or of anybody in power?

_____

_____

_____

_____

_____

_____

_____

2. Isaiah 5:1–13. What does the comparison (parable/story/song) do that might have been missed had the facts been stated straight?

_____

_____

_____

_____

_____

_____

_____

3. Matthew 7:28–29; 13:10–17 and 34–35; Luke 9:44. What was being hidden, what was being revealed, to whom, and why?

_____

_____

_____

_____

_____

_____

_____

_____

4. Which stories have made an impact on your life, and why? Which story from this week's readings speaks to you most? Why?

_____

_____

_____

_____

_____

_____

_____

5. What stories could you tell that might speak to different people in the school mentioned at the end of Opening Our Eyes?

_____

_____

_____

_____

_____

_____

_____

Personal Application

What people do you know who are enemies of the gospel? Who do you know who'd be delighted to be 'liberated' but has the wrong idea about what liberation means? Do you know anyone who has been put off by being told the truth before he or she was ready – inoculated against the gospel, as it were? Do you know any faithful disciple of Jesus (yourself perhaps?) who ever gets the wrong idea about what He wants, or what He stands for? Jesus' stories revealed and concealed truth for all those types of people in a way that 'straight' teaching could never have done. Living His stories, learning to tell stories as He did, so that they take on a life of their own, and maybe make sense only later in time – that's a real challenge! Ask for His help.

Seeing Jesus in the Scriptures

Reading Matthew 13:10–15, how do you see Jesus? As very hard? I see that passage as meaning that people judge themselves by their reaction to Jesus and His parables. Saddened, He knows that some will never change. For others, if His truth comes at them sideways it may have a chance to percolate gently into their imagination, easing them gently from being stuck with their wrong perceptions. Then maybe they will be ready to accept Him as their Saviour.

WEEK 2

Parables told to the crowd

Opening Icebreaker and Worship

When you've sat listening to speakers, what in their communication worked best – and worst? Their personality, credentials, presentation skills, the illustrations, the relevance?

Communicating effectively with many people, each one of whom may be very different from the others, isn't easy. Focus your worship, wonder and thanks on God who communicates with millions of different cultures around the world. His Word communicates across the millennia too! Ask Him to speak to you as you do this study together.

Bible Readings

- Matthew 5:13–16; 7:1–27; 13:1–9; 13:24–35
- John 6:25–59

Opening Our Eyes

How did Jesus communicate with the crowd through parables? To help answer that we'll employ the journalist's five faithful questions – who, where, when, why, what?

Who were the crowd? Mainly the poor, 'ordinary' people who saw Jesus healing and working other miracles, heard Him proclaiming God's kingdom was coming and thus saw in Him a hope where they'd had none before. It wasn't simply that God's 'chosen people' were suffering oppressive Roman occupation in the land they'd been promised. Herod, placed by the Romans in charge of them, was corrupt. He'd given the best land to his rich chums – absentee landlords who made extortionate demands on tenant farmers. The ordinary people were taxed by Romans and the priestly system of tithing had spiralled out of hand too. Many tradesmen, carpenters for example, also lived below the breadline, meaning that the great majority of Israel's people were desperate – and their God seemed to be doing nothing. Many were asking, wasn't Jesus the revolutionary One, promised and anointed by God to restore His justice to the kingdom?

Where were the crowds? Following Jesus in the open air (the only space big enough) – by a lake shore, on the slopes of a hill …

When did He talk to the ordinary, poor people, to the crowd? Some theologians suggest mostly at the start of His ministry – and that He concentrated effort on His disciples later. That's not what I find in my Bible!

Why was He communicating with them? Part of the answer is because they wouldn't go away. They'd been so attracted by what He did and how He lived that they were full of hopeful questions about who He was and what He would do. Jesus had compassion on them, He wanted to show them the way to the Father. But He had to be careful that they didn't get the wrong idea. A crowd is more than a collection of individuals. It can develop a powerful force of its own. He couldn't let them think of Him as some fiery revolutionary, one who might incite them to guerrilla-style violence or as one who asked His Father to zap all the 'baddies' with thunderbolts.

What did Jesus talk about? Often the things they could see, or everyday things in their lives – He rarely touched on anything 'religious' and His stories can be taken at face value as wise words about this world. But, for those with eyes to see, there is more. His main topic for the crowd was the kingdom of heaven. He said it grew slowly – like a seed, was one illustration. God was working, how He was working, for those with eyes to see! He still cared desperately about the poor, about justice, righteousness and mercy, about the way people behaved – towards one another and towards Him. He was doing something very new, very revolutionary, but it was a revolution of love and, because it was taking place in people's hearts and not by force, it would work surely
… but slowly.

So – to whom, where, when, why and what are you and I communicating? To crowds? With small groups such as a hobby-club, Parent-Teacher Association, our work colleagues? With 'ordinary', perhaps marginalised people? Remembering the importance of Jesus' great commission to 'make disciples of all nations' (people-groups), 'teaching them to obey everything I have commanded you' (Matt. 28:18–20), let's have a closer look at His preferred way of teaching lots of people – parables!

Discussion Starters

1. Matthew 5:13–16 follows on from the Beatitudes –
how do these two short 'parables' also turn everything
upside down
a) for the poor people in the crowd?

_____

_____

b) for you?

_____

_____

c) do they have anything to say to those who don't
know Jesus?

_____

_____

2. Matthew 7:1–29 (the same crowd is being addressed).
How is Jesus communicating? Think about pace,
humour and hyperbole (exaggeration). What
references does He use? Find examples of comparison,
shock, warning, encouragement, picture, memorable
'sound bite' and of questions He provokes. What
answers might He be giving to the crowd's unrecorded
questions? How does He draw in his hearers even with
these ultra-short stories, helping them to identify with
what He's talking about, encouraging them to use their
own imagination? Where is He asking them to think
'outside of the box' – to change their perceptions?

_____

_____

_____

Why did they think He taught 'as one who had
authority, and not as their teachers of the law'?

_____

_____

_____

_____

_____

3. Matthew 13:1–9. According to Stephen Wright in *Tales Jesus Told*, Jesus was addressing poor farmers whose land had been stripped from them so they were forced to grow their seed on marginal land – around edges, paths, stony places, thorn-bushes ... You're one of those farmers in the crowd. You've never heard Jesus' explanation to His disciples, never heard this story before, let alone heard anyone preaching on it. What does it mean to you? Are you wondering why Jesus is telling you about it – whether there is more to His words than meets the eye?

_____

_____

_____

4. Matthew 13:24–35. The mustard shrub is not the biggest of 'trees' and the Jewish religion saw yeast as a symbol of bad influence spoiling the good – how is Jesus subverting people's set thought patterns here?

_____

_____

_____

What questions might the story of the wheat and weeds answer
(a) for the crowd?

_____

_____

(b) for the churched and un-churched today?

_____

_____

Personal Application

Following on from Discussion Starter 4, what are the
eternal truths today which centuries of distorted thinking
and layers of empty religion have hidden? How might
we startle people into seeing clearly again?

Parables gain more power because they aren't dogma
or rigid rules which fit one place and one time alone.
Instead they allow their truth to be revealed in different
ways at different times to different people. What in
particular has the Holy Spirit helped you to see in a new
light through the parables we've just been exploring?

Seeing Jesus in the Scriptures

We can learn a great deal about people from the stories
they tell, and the way they tell them. What can you learn
about Jesus from the stories He told to the crowd? As
we're now His Body, including His mouth and voice on
earth, how can we learn from Him to communicate not
just the facts or the stories, but the Person behind the
facts and the stories? Knowing Him, can we make (and
live) fresh stories which will bring glory, not to ourselves,
but to Him?

WEEK 3

Parables told to friends and disciples

Opening Icebreaker and Worship

Share about a time when a close Christian friend, answering your question, has helped you 'see' something helpful.

Worshipping God with a small group of Christians who regularly build up and disciple one another is very special. If you're in such a group now, worship God in a way you find appropriate – perhaps in response to the picture-parables in Luke 12:6–7.

Bible Readings

Select some from:
- Luke 11:5–13; 16:1–15; 18:1–8
- Mark 4:10–34
- Matthew 13:34–50; 25:1–46

Opening Our Eyes

Counting Jesus' parables recorded in the Bible, I found by far the most were told to His disciples, then to the crowd, then to His enemies – and the least in response to individuals, to the rich, the powerful and the nation as a whole. In this study we can't hope to cover all the parables that Jesus told to His friends. Even the reduced list above would keep you occupied for several sessions – so choose some readings from it and look at others at home. If you want a challenge, perhaps the most difficult of all parables are the first two on the list. Considering who Jesus was addressing has helped me understand them.

Of the millions of words Jesus must have spoken to His disciples, they perhaps remembered His story-answers best. So, how did Jesus communicate through parables told to His friends and disciples? How were they different from the ones He told the crowd?

Jesus told parables in response to questions from His disciples. These men and women had left everything to follow Jesus – and they spent hours with Him, eating meals, some walking the length of their country at His side. He was their Rabbi; some came to believe Him their Messiah – of course they asked Him questions. Some are recorded (Matt. 13:36; Mark 9:34: Luke 11:1), others implicit. Most are no different from awkward ones we hear or ask today: 'Why doesn't God deal with injustice?' 'Why can't we see it, if this kingdom You keep talking about is among us?' 'How are we to live when You're not with us in the flesh any more?' and 'How should we prepare for Your return?'

Jesus normally refers to the everyday life of His time in His parables, so it helps us to know a little about it. And, as conflict fuels all stories, it's important to know in what areas Jesus was provoking a battle for God's kingdom of love and righteousness. For example, God's heart, as shown by the whole sweep of Scripture, is for the poor. Yet archaeologists have found remains of opulent houses belonging to Jewish priests of Jesus' era. These priests were teaching that wealth showed God's blessing: poverty His curse. They lacked compassion for the sufferings of the ordinary people, most of whom lived below the breadline. Take that into account when reading Luke 16:1–15 and you might get a message consistent with that given to the rich young ruler (18:18–25): 'Riches mess you up whether you're the owner or the manager – better to give them away, just as you, My disciples, have given everything!'

An unjust judge (Luke 18:1–8) was considered the worst of men – the butt of many a joke. The Old Testament teaches that whoever doesn't fear God is a fool. This is Jesus' 'Have you heard the one about …' It's also a 'How much more …' story told, I'm sure, with a wry smile. If a fool of an unjust judge can be stirred into action by a nagging widow, how much more will God hear your prayers and act!

The 'treasures new and old' (Matt. 13:52) can't have been easy even for Jesus' closest friends to assimilate – and they probably have the same effect on us. At least, whenever I read these stories, God jumps out of yet another 'box' in which I've attempted to contain Him. Are you prepared to be surprised, even shocked, by Jesus?

Discussion Starters

1. Luke 16:1–15. Remember Jesus was speaking to disciples who had given up everything to follow Him, overheard by Pharisees who believed wealth a sign of God's blessing. How is Jesus using shock tactics in His storytelling to make them think again?

What question of the disciples might Jesus have been answering here?

2. Luke 18:1–8. Again, what question of the disciples might Jesus be answering here? Have you heard, or asked, a similar question recently?

How would you answer someone? Does Luke 11:5–13 help?

3. Look at the parables of the sower and of the weeds as told first to the crowd. Then decide what extra points is Jesus making for His disciples – and why (Matt. 13:36–43; Mark 4:14–20). Again, what questions of the disciples may have prompted Him?

What stories or comparisons would you make or tell to answer similar questions from new-ish Christians today?

4. In the light of Jesus' words about seeds growing secretly (Mark 4:26–29), about pearls and treasure (Matt. 13:44–46), can you think of similar mini-sagas or picture-language to express your sense of His Kingdom's joy and mystery to one another?

_____

_____

What do you feel about the different note sounded in the parable of the dragnet (Matt. 13:47–50)?

_____

_____

5. Think about the point in Jesus' ministry in which He told His disciples the parables in Matthew 25. How does that help you understand their meaning?

_____

_____

What stories would you leave with friends if you were about to die?

_____

_____

If you were about to go away for several years, how might you communicate to prepare any Christians you're discipling?

_____

_____

Thinking about the parables of the talents, what wrong understanding of God's character underlies the actions of the man who refused to take a risk with his one talent – and do you ever find yourselves in a similar position?

_____

_____

Personal Application

Does the way you answer friends' questions about Jesus engage their imagination and cause them to get to know Him more? If you are regaling them with the kind of stock Christian answers which shut Jesus in a box (not a pill, but a verse for every ill) think instead what wondrous stories you have to tell about Him. And how the Holy Spirit has helped you picture the immense riches of eternity.

Seeing Jesus in the Scriptures

There's Jesus, in all our readings this week, relating intimately with His closest friends. Who did they see? They saw more than us, yet understood surprisingly little of the Person He was at that stage. What blocked their vision? What blocks yours?

Radical truths take a while to penetrate human consciousness. Maybe that's why Jesus used stories and picture-language so much – they stay in the mind and work on the imagination, on the spirit even.

My grandmother lived with us when I was a child but has been dead now for years. I remember – and reconsider her now I'm an adult – largely through her oft-repeated stories. The stories people choose to tell show us a great deal about the person they are. What do you see of Jesus' character in these stories which have intrigued, inspired or infuriated people for so many generations? Have you seen anything new or surprising as you've thought, discussed, read and prayed your way through this study? Ask the Holy Spirit to help you see, love and obey Jesus even more clearly.

WEEK 4

Parables told to enemies

Opening Icebreaker and Worship

How do you communicate with people whose thoughts, beliefs, loves, and so on, are completely different from your own? If you've managed to turn round a negative interaction with someone, tell the group how you did it.

We've all fought God at times. That we can worship Him now is amazing. Read or sing the words of one of the great hymns which expresses that – 'Amazing Grace' perhaps. Then read Luke 15:1–32, sensing the 'out-of-all-proportion' joy God feels when someone lost is found.

Bible Readings

- Luke 15:1–32; 16:19–31; 18:9–14
- Matthew 21:23–22:22

Opening Our Eyes

We're looking at conflict. Who has authority? And what kind of authority?

In a heated argument with people who hold completely different values from yourself, would you tell stories? Jesus' stories told to such people are among the best-known, loved and re-told of all His parables. They didn't win over most of His enemies then but have inspired many people to change over the years and still confront the attitudes of those of us keen on obedience to God, on holiness, on attending every religious service going.

Jesus told the three 'lost' stories when religious types criticised Him for keeping company with sinners. Has anyone in your church ever been criticised for doing the same thing? Although we're considering Jesus addressing His enemies, we can't relax into self-righteousness. These stories are radical. Jesus asked if they would leave 99 sheep to look for one lost one? The answer is, no. It wouldn't make economic sense for a responsible shepherd. The wandering shepherds then had the bad reputation of being uncaring thieves. Jesus' hearers, though, knew this wasn't about men, good or bad, but about God, Israel's Good Shepherd. Religious Jews believed God welcomed repentant sinners, but was far too 'holy' to seek them out actively – making the 'lost son' story outrageous. A father *running* to meet a good son then was shockingly undignified – let alone one fresh from a pigsty (pigs being the great Jewish taboo). All three stories end with amazing rejoicing when the lost is found. By contrast, religious people, who prefer criticising rather than celebrating others, mirror the older brother who misses out on the party and all the good things which are his already. He's become too small to give love or to cope with grace.

In the story of the rich man and Lazarus, Jesus challenged another deeply-held belief – that 'unrighteous' Jews would suffer in Hades for 12 months before Abraham came to restore them to their birthright at his side. Lazarus means 'God is my help'. Jesus' enemies believed poverty to be a judgment of God: Jesus was saying God's passion is to help the poor.

Jesus told the parable of the Pharisee and the tax collector, 'to those who were confident of their own righteousness and looked down on everybody else' (Luke 18:9). Do His words remind you of how Christians are perceived – not without reason sometimes? Jesus was being so provocative. Jews who came anywhere near the Temple were supposed to pray there twice a day. The Pharisee, according to Ruth Etchells in *A Reading of the Parables of Jesus*, spoke the prescribed words for praying out loud, so he wasn't inventing his own self-righteousness.

The parables in our Matthew reading come in response to Temple priests and elders questioning Jesus' authority. Replying to one question with another can be good strategy. After His comparison-parable question, Jesus goes on the attack, with stories for weapons. 'You don't obey God: the people you dub vile sinners do.' 'Left in charge of God's vineyard, instead of giving Him the fruit, you've beaten His messengers, killed His heir … God will take from you, giving to the once-rejected.' The next parable comes to similar shocking conclusions, employing humour – what daft excuses for not coming to the feast! Lastly, another enemy question is answered by another comparison-parable question, involving the visual aid of a coin.

The underlying question in all of this (who has authority?) is answered neatly when Jesus' enemies walk away, unable to say or do anything further – an acted out, real-life parable.

Discussion Starters

1. Luke 15:1–32. Do you, and your church, take risks to find people who are lost? When someone is found, what is the reaction – extravagant joy or worry about the messy consequences?

_____
_____
_____
_____

What can you learn from God's rejoicing over small things?

_____
_____
_____
_____

2. Luke 16:19–31. What is your attitude to the poor?

_____
_____
_____
_____

3. Luke 18:9–14. Do you consider 'those who are confident of their own righteousness and look down on everybody else' are enemies of God? What happens if any one group (in power) is arrogant enough to think that way?

_____
_____
_____
_____

What, at the time, was the shock value of this parable?

_____

_____

_____

4. Matthew 21:23–22:22. Does Jesus' authority ever conflict with church (or civil) authority? How can 'ordinary' Christians find a godly way through the moral maze if it does?

_____

_____

_____

_____

What can we learn from Jesus in this passage about communicating with people in authority?

_____

_____

_____

_____

Personal Application

How do you handle conflict – especially conflict caused by your faith? How do you feel when you tell your stories of Jesus' work in your own life and people turn away, seemingly more entrenched in their position? Have you counted the cost?

Who has authority in your life? For example, you see a neighbour in need just at that time on a Sunday when you would normally be going to church – and no one else can, or will, help. What does the love of Christ compel you to do (2 Cor. 5:14)?

Seeing Jesus in the Scriptures

As well as being provocative, I see Jesus trying to help those people who had become stuck. To escape from an entrenched position you first have to imagine something different – and better. I wonder if Jesus' stories helped any of them to do that? We're not told either way, though there are hints that some Pharisees, priests and rabbis did become Christians. How could you follow Him in this 're-imagining' ministry? What else do you learn from the way He dialogues with these people? What makes these parables so memorable?

WEEK 5

Parables told to individuals who asked questions

Opening Icebreaker and Worship

When was the last time someone (not from church) asked you a question about God? What did you reply?

Lay your honest questions before God in silence, ask the Holy Spirit to speak to you, then be quiet a few more minutes, listening for His response. If anyone senses something and doesn't understand, share it – it may illuminate something for another person. Pray together, giving Him praise for who He is.

Bible Readings

- Mark 2:15–22
- Luke 7:36–50; 10:25–37 cf. 2 Chronicles 28:14–15
- Matthew 18:21–35

Opening Our Eyes

'When your children ask you … say …', so goes the refrain in the Old Testament. That's how Jewish parents taught their children about God – they provoked questions. Jesus provoked numerous questions, often from individuals. How often do we provoke anyone into asking questions about Jesus?

In our first reading, Jesus' behaviour provoked 'some people' into questioning Him about fasting or feasting. Then the Pharisees asked – how could a rabbi party, especially with such wicked people? For 400 years previously the prophets remained silent and now the nation was over-run and impoverished in every way – spiritually, materially, in leadership … The whole nation was in mourning. Good Jews should be fasting as God continued to punish their sin. They hadn't seen that Jesus' coming brought extraordinary, and unexpected, changes. He came as Saviour – and what ordinary, everyday examples He chose to illustrate the cosmic shift now He had arrived!

In our second reading, the question Jesus answered wasn't put to Him directly – but He read Simon the Pharisee's reaction and answered it anyway. How could He, a rabbi, let a shameless woman kiss His feet, pour costly perfume on them, then wipe them with her hair? Perhaps Jesus knew that this woman offered Him pure love, born of repentance, but it looked the kind of thing prostitutes would do – a sexual act. Wouldn't we ask questions if our minister allowed a 'loose woman' to treat him like this at a church supper? Jesus raised the temperature to boiling by claiming to forgive sins and then shaming Simon for his lukewarm welcome.

A teacher of the law asks Jesus a test-question and appears to know the correct answer. Jesus tells the Good

Samaritan story to confound his complacency. Even though they originated from the ten tribes of the former Northern Kingdom (known as Israel) Samaritans weren't nice people according to the Jerusalem Jews (the tribes of Judah and Benjamin). None so suspect as those who have been 'one of us' and then split off on a different (especially theological) road. The reason the traveller took the bandit-ridden Jericho road from Jerusalem was most probably to avoid apostate Samaria on his way north. What I've never before seen – but Stephen Wright points out in *Tales Jesus Told* – is the amazing way Jesus' story echoes Chronicles. His hearers would have known the story. King Ahaz of Judah had done evil in the sight of the Lord. Israel (capital: Samaria) had been an agent of God's punishment, but had gone too far both in the massacre and in taking prisoner-slaves, so the prophet Obed tells them to act ... well, like the Good Samaritan.

The 12 apostles were a quarrelsome bunch, according to the Gospels. In our final reading, Peter clearly felt justified in asking how often he must forgive his brother. Did Jesus ever doubt that His closest friends, in whom He invested so much, would ever embrace His message? His response wasn't gentle. Ever heard anyone exaggerate, to pull someone up short when they are being petty, perhaps? The 10,000 talents of the story was – still is – an unimaginably large sum of money. And an unimaginably enormous amount is what we owe God compared to what any human being owes us, even if he or she has wronged us 490 plus times. Grace comes to us free, not cheap. Jesus paid the extraordinary price.

The more I read the Gospels, the more I see that Jesus' big battle was convincing people that God wanted to include, not exclude, others from His kingdom – even those whose many sins made them appear unforgivable. The consequences raise all kinds of questions. Are you ready?

Discussion Starters

1. Mark 2:15–22. How does believing Jesus is the Saviour radically alter your behaviour and the people you mix with?

How do you express the difference Jesus makes?

2. Luke 7:36–50. How would you have reacted, had you been a fellow guest of Simon's?

How do Jesus' answers, in word and deed, communicate the radical nature of His love and of the good news He brings to those who have ears to hear?

3. Luke 10:25–37; 2 Chronicles 28:14–15. Who today do people exclude as 'beyond the pale', beyond God's grace? Do any Christians you know exclude other kinds of Christians?

_____
_____

What stories could you tell to help them see with a more God's-eye view?

_____
_____
_____
_____

4. Matthew 18:21–35. We all have 'blind spots' and Jesus was faithful to His friends, telling them stories which would catch their conscience and help them see again. Has your conscience ever been caught by a story, or by a comparison?

_____
_____
_____
_____

How would you explain the unexplainable – that is, grace?

_____
_____
_____
_____

5. How could we provoke our children into asking more questions about God – and how can we best respond when they ask difficult or surprising ones?

_____
_____
_____
_____

Personal Application

When people ask you questions about God or your faith, do you, like me, come up with brilliant answers – two or three days later? Let's listen out for the kind of questions people are asking. Are they the ones we hear the answers to in church? Even more importantly, let's ask the Holy Spirit to keep us in tune with Himself, just as Jesus was, so that we actually find ourselves saying the right thing at the right time, with real insight, truth and life. We could even ask Him for some stories!

When He inspires us and people actually see something of the gospel for the first time, it's amazing! But don't be disheartened if they remain blind. Even with Jesus it took time – and some of the questioners turned away with hardened hearts. In the end it took His life. Our lives too speak louder than our words, provoking questions in the first place. What in your life is provoking questions about Him?

Seeing Jesus in the Scriptures

Jesus is very human here, as He responds to puzzled, 'disgusted' or hostile questions from individuals or small groups. He seems very alone in seeing, let alone living, His Father's truth on earth. As He communicates, He Himself becomes the way, the truth and the life for these people. Or He could be, would they but listen – and do and be as He says.

WEEK | **SIX**

WEEK 6

Parables told to the rich and powerful, or the nation

Opening Icebreaker and Worship

Who is the most important, influential or wealthy person you can think of? Why did you choose that particular man or woman?

Worship means 'to give worth to'. We could never make Jesus worth more than He is now but we can still worship Him – He who has all riches, power and authority, who alone is worthy to be worshipped. To worship such a One changes us – especially if we do so creatively, using the gifts He's given us individually and as a group.

Bible Readings

• Luke 7:1–10; 12:13–34; 13:1–9,31–35; 18:18–30

39

Opening Our Eyes

In Luke 7:1–10 we start, not with a parable told by Jesus to someone in power, but with one told *to* Jesus by the officer commanding 100 soldiers of the army occupying God's land and ruling over God's people. Amazingly, the centurion makes the same point as Jesus' parables: that true power (and riches) belong, not to elite human beings, nor to nations, but to God. This centurion, unusual in that 'he loves our nation and has built our synagogue' reveres the Jewish God but, unlike the Jewish religious leaders, actually recognises God's authority in Jesus. Astounding! Drawing a parallel with the workings of his own authority he's certain that, if Jesus gives the word, his servant will be healed.

There's power in riches too … or is there? In Luke 12:13–34, two brothers in dispute over a legacy (they weren't poor, then!) ask Jesus to take authority and judge between them. He refuses and tells a story revealing their foolishness. No one was an atheist in those days. 'The fool says in his heart, "There is no God" ' (Psa. 14:1; 53:1), means that a fool acts as though God has no part in his life. The picture-parables Jesus tells His followers are about how they can live with God as Kingly provider. How different from those subject to an earthly kingdom where they think human beings are in charge.

In Luke 18:18–30 again we see pictures illustrating the differences between those who rely on wealth and power and those who give up everything to follow Jesus. Camels going through needles' eyes sounds so extreme we're not surprised when the hearers ask who on earth can be saved? W.E.O. Oesterley in *The Gospel Parables in the Light of their Jewish Background* quotes the ancient saying, 'Thou has presumably come from Pumbeditha where they can make an elephant go through the eye of a needle', explaining that Pumbeditha was a centre of Jewish scholarship in Babylonia. If that saying was in Jesus' mind, was He criticising Jewish teachers who could squeeze and twist God's Word so as to make Him seem to prefer and bless the rich above the poor?

Things don't change much, do they? We hear the same questions today as people were asking in Jesus' time. 'If God's who He says He is, why did He let X happen?' (X being the latest atrocity or disaster to hit the headlines.) In Luke 13:1–9 we see that Pontius Pilate, prone to attacking his subjects at the merest hint of rebellion, slaughtered a group of Jews as they worshipped God with sacrifices in the Temple. 'Massacre in Holiest Sanctuary!' today's headlines might scream. Others were killed in an accident. Where was God? Why didn't He act? 'Clearly,' replied the religious Jews, 'the worst baddies had to die.' See how Jesus used stories in the news, and religious authorities' mistaken speculation about them, to bring out the truth that *everyone* needed to repent! The Jewish people were being given one last chance to do so before God brought judgment.

Luke 13:31–35; have you heard the one about the fox and the chickens? Herod was an upstart, appointed by the Romans. Jesus treats that fox's threats with the contempt they deserve. Then we hear His anguish in knowing His country-folk's intransigence can only lead to their destruction. His authority becomes as vulnerable as that of a mother hen, who would die defending her chicks – except most won't even now run to Him for shelter.

Discussion Starters

1. Luke 7:1–10. We've talked about Jesus' parables surprising and even shocking His hearers. Why is Jesus Himself so amazed here?

_____

_____

_____

_____

_____

Control issues are at the forefront of many a debate in today's world. What can you learn about right authority from the centurion's attitude?

_____

_____

_____

_____

_____

2. Luke 12:13–34. Why, if Jesus has authority, does He tell parables instead of judging between the brothers in their dispute?

_____

_____

_____

_____

_____

3. Luke 18:18–30. What can you learn from this and the previous passage about how to speak to those with money and power – and to 'ordinary' godly people who appear to have little? What tone of voice do you think Jesus would have used in verses 22–24?

_____

_____

_____

_____
_____

4. Luke 13:1–9. 'What if ...' is a good storytelling question. What fruits might the tree have borne had all Israel repented? What if the Church all followed Christ fully – throughout history ... and now?

_____
_____
_____
_____
_____
_____

5. Luke 13:31–35. Assuming that the Pharisees mentioned were genuine in wanting to warn Jesus of real danger, what do you learn from His parable-pictures about how to respond in such a situation?

_____
_____
_____
_____
_____
_____

Personal Application

Compared with the poor of Jesus' time, most of us, in the West, are unimaginably wealthy and wield considerable power – so these parables are very applicable to us! In what practical ways can we use our power and wealth for the kingdom, as the Roman centurion did? What are the pitfalls and dangers of doing so … and of having wealth and power? When I returned from visiting an amazing church in Ghana, I felt like moving into our garden shed. What more practical steps could we take to live differently, more simply, relying more on God?

Seeing Jesus in the Scriptures

Anger, sorrow, wonder, compassion, provocation, contempt (of wrong), humour, awareness, courage, obedience to God, humility, spiritual insight – what else of Jesus' heart can you see in these passages? It seems to me we see the best of humanity here in Jesus, who was fully human, as He is fully divine – His life a picture parable in which we really do see 'God with us' as well as a pattern for our own worship and behaviour.

WEEK 7

'I will open my mouth in parables'

Opening Icebreaker and Worship

What's the best short sermon illustration you've ever heard – and what made it so memorable?

Spend a few moments in silence, each asking God to let you see more of different aspects of Himself. Then ask Him to give you the words or picture, the dance or song in which to express those things back to Him in worship.

Bible Readings

- Psalm 78:1–8, 70–72
- Mark 9:35–37; 10:13–16; 11:12–14, 20–21; 13:28–29
- Matthew 15:21–28; 20:1–16
- Luke 19:11–27

Opening Our Eyes

'I will open my mouth in parables, I will utter hidden things, things from of old … we will tell the next generation the praiseworthy deeds of the LORD.' So begins Psalm 78, which ends with the metaphor of David chosen by God to 'shepherd' His people (does this remind you of Jesus' words to Peter in John 21:16–17?).

Parables, stories and metaphors, rather than proof texts, formulae and commandments, are the main means through which the Bible – and Jesus – communicate with us. They've been re-told, in art and literature, countless times down the ages. The eternal truths embedded within them have been re-interpreted through the everyday details of life in different cultures, centuries, seasons. They are our tools to spread the good news about Jesus.

What kind of parables might we tell? Mini-sagas perhaps, based on the things we see around us. We may not be in regular contact with fig trees or mountains by the seaside but I've heard individuals drawing brilliant analogies about the kingdom of God from the workings of a football team – or from a multi-level motorway junction. What ordinary things around you might speak of things eternal? I'm currently having treatment for an injury that's left me with a 'frozen shoulder'. The physiotherapist keeps apologising for hurting me but, if he doesn't, I'll lose the use of my right arm. I'm thinking that's a bit like us, sin-damaged, needing to squeeze through the narrow gate, taking the difficult path before we reach the wide place God always intended for us. Or like the pain of a seed falling to the ground and dying before it can grow and bear fruit. Ask God to show you 'parable parallels'. Tell them to one another and to those who don't yet know God.

Sometimes these everyday analogies may shock people. Jesus' attitude to little children seems all sweet and cosy to us, but His was an age where children counted for nothing, were powerless, had no rights and often died young. Jesus' reversed attitude pulls the disciples up sharp as they argue about who is greatest – but a little later He has to make the same point again when they are stopping children approaching Him. Interestingly, Matthew's Good Shepherd parable (18:12–14) also comes in the context of valuing children. Learning comes through repetition – and reminders work best when seen every day.

And then there's Christian brainwashing. Well, didn't (doesn't) Jesus use parables among other things to power-hose away widely held misconceptions, turning them upside down, replacing them with a heaven's eye view? For example: Universal cry: 'It's not fair!' Universal truth: Life isn't fair! Jesus' new slant: 'Grace isn't fair!' Expect God to be fair rather than full of grace and we're in real trouble. Jesus almost always used everyday rather than 'religious' examples to demonstrate points like this. Men, deprived of their land and desperate for work, would hang around all day in marketplaces, hoping to be hired for a few hours at harvest time. Laws of supply and demand meant hirers weren't generous, normally. Do our language and our examples of heaven touching earth, like Jesus', make sense to everyone, not just to religious types?

God seems to love parables and stories – so can we tell them to Him? Well, the Canaanite woman told a parable as she was praying for help for her daughter and it appeared to make Jesus change His mind, for up to this point He seemed to believe He was called to minister to His own people.

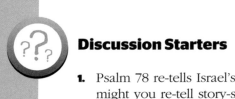

Discussion Starters

1. Psalm 78 re-tells Israel's salvation history with God. How might you re-tell story-sized chunks of your personal, group or church salvation history which will intrigue, interest or somehow chime with people you meet?

_____

_____

_____

_____

_____

_____

2. Mark 11:12–14, 20–21, 13:28–9. What mini-sagas or riddles could you tell to illuminate something of God – or to get people intrigued about spiritual matters in the first place?

_____

_____

_____

_____

_____

_____

3. Mark 9:35–37; 10:13–16. In many countries, attitudes to children have become more like Jesus'. Which people-groups are not treated in a Christlike manner in your community and country?

_____

_____

_____

_____

_____

_____

Can you imagine something different – and live, as
well as tell, God-stories involving them?

_____
_____
_____
_____
_____
_____

4. Matthew 20:1–16. What misconceived truths do you
come across most often concerning God and His
kingdom – both in and outside the Church?

_____
_____
_____
_____
_____
_____

What stories could you tell to show that things might
be different?

_____
_____
_____
_____
_____
_____

5. Luke 19:11–26. Have you ever prayed a parable,
or told God a story?

_____
_____
_____
_____
_____
_____

Personal Application

To understand the Bible properly we need to understand the culture, the landscape, the history. To live in the light of what the Bible says we need to become part of its story – and we do that by walking in close relationship with God, listening to, obeying and drawing strength from Him and allowing the Holy Spirit to lead us into all truth. To communicate alive God-truth to Christians and non-Christians around us today we need to do all that and then re-interpret, finding new images and stories for our times.

Seeing Jesus in the Scriptures

What I see in these stories is the doing, the actions in parallel with the saying, the teaching. Jesus' whole life illustrated His message. He came to show us what God is like. He said if we have seen Him we've seen the Father. Then He died and rose again, bearing 'much fruit' – we can see Jesus reflected in the lives of so many we read about in the rest of the New Testament, in later biographies of Christians and in those who love Him today. Let's pray that our lives too are a godly parable – that if people see, hear and touch us, they'll see, hear and touch a little bit of Jesus!

Leader's Notes

Material you may find helpful

There are many books, and sections within books, about the parables. A few caused me to wonder if the author's Bible was a completely different book from mine! Books I found most helpful (in order) were:

Michael Ball, *The Radical Stories of Jesus: Interpreting the Parables Today* (Oxford: Regent's Park College, 2000). Not easy to get hold of but invaluable. I ordered it through the college www.rpc.ox.ac.uk

Ruth Etchells, *A Reading of the Parables of Jesus* (Darton, Longman and Todd, 1998).

Stephen I. Wright, *Tales Jesus Told: an introduction to the narrative parables of Jesus* (Paternoster, 2002). The same author/publisher produced in 2000 *The Voice of Jesus: Studies in the interpretation of six Gospel parables.*

Tom Wright, *Matthew/Mark/Luke for Everyone* (SPCK separate volumes, early 2000s).

W.E.O. Oesterley, *The Gospel Parables in the Light of their Jewish Background* (SPCK, 1936).

Week 1: To hide and to reveal: parables and their uses

Opening Icebreaker and Worship

The cloth should cover some receptacle, such as a lidded box. Inside the box you can place whatever your imagination sees as fit. You could even wrap it in some paper. Ask, 'Do you want to know what's inside?' If people are intrigued by what is hidden, get them to talk briefly about why they feel like that. If this group is a new group, perhaps brought together short-term to look at this study guide, make time for introductions and for people to get to know each other.

For the worship you could sing a hymn or Christian song, play one on CD or tape or simply read the words together – and then spend time in prayer.

Aim of the Session
To introduce people to the not-so-simple subject of parables, the variety of ways in which they were, are and could be used.

You may well find there is too much material and too many Bible passages for the group to discuss and pray over within any one week. As group leader you will probably want to read them through beforehand and decide which passages and which questions would suit your group best. Or you could devote more than one group session to one or more particular 'Weeks' in the book.

Some other interesting Old Testament parables are Judges 9:7–15; 2 Samuel 14:3; 2 Kings 14:9–10; Proverbs 24:30–34; Ezekiel 17.

Discussion Starters
1: Two well-known examples are:
a) Charles Dickens became so concerned about conditions in which the poor of London were living that he was going to write a pamphlet called *An Approach to the People of England on Behalf of the Poor Man's Child*. Fortunately, he wrote *A Christmas Carol* instead; it caught people's imagination and made a real difference.
b) The television play, *Cathy Come Home*, awakened the nation to the plight of the homeless – which still isn't solved, but the charity Shelter and other initiatives began as a result.

2. There are several right answers to this question. Personally I'm moved by the way the story reveals God's heart, His emotion, His love and His hurt.

Week 2: Parables told to the crowd

Opening Icebreaker and Worship

Try to limit the discussion to ten minutes – and to get people thinking along the lines not so much of what was said but how it was communicated effectively (or ineffectively).

Aim of the Session

A 'How To'. How to communicate Jesus' great commission (Matt. 28:18–20)!

I have used Matthew's Gospel almost exclusively in this section simply because, within it, a number of parables addressed to the crowd follow on very nicely one from another. In other Gospels some parables are addressed to different people (salt, light and mustard seed to the disciples in Mark; narrow/wide ways to an individual in Luke). That doesn't mean the Bible contradicts itself. Jesus may well have repeated the same story or saying in different contexts – or maybe one Gospel writer was more interested in the effect the storytelling had on an individual, another on Jesus' enemies or disciples, all of whom might well have been present in the crowd.

Parallel passages are: sower Mark 4:1–9, Luke 8:4–8; salt Mark 9:50; Luke 14:34 and light Luke 11:33–6; plank Luke 6:41–42; narrow/wide Luke 13:24–25; fruit Luke 6:43–45, see also Matthew 12:33; house on rock Matthew 7:24; mustard seed Luke 13:18; yeast Luke 13:20. John's Gospel has no parables as such but is rich in imagery and the seven signs are acted-out parables – look at John 6 if you want to see one for the crowd.

Discussion Starters

1. Salt was used to purify food (and symbolically in Temple sacrifices – Leviticus 2:13). People of Jesus' time, living in a hot country, would have know that consuming the then-precious commodity, salt, was vital to life. It was mined from rock or gleaned from evaporation. Because it wasn't pure sodium chloride its 'saltiness' could leach out and sometimes the residue might be used 'underfoot' to prevent people slipping over (think of icy roads gritted with rock-salt today).

Light is equally vital for life. Much light shines from a city at night. God intended hilltop Jerusalem (and Israel) to be a light for the nations. Or perhaps Jesus was pointing to a smaller hilltop town that the crowd could see. Com-munities may shine but even the weak light from one oil lamp is important. Each 'ordinary' person within the crowd – the poor in spirit, the mourners, the meek, pure, merciful, the hungry, thirsty and persecuted – is vital. They can't be hidden or spoilt, except by their own choice. God will work through them, in ways big or small, to light and purify His world.

2. Matthew 7:24–29 is one of those stories I thought I'd understood since I was three! It was only from Ruth Etchell's book *A Reading of the Parables of Jesus* that I 'saw' a house built on the sandy land of a wadi – a normally dry desert valley engulfed by a powerfully destructive torrent during a cloudburst. She also helped me hear strong echoes of Noah and of Isaiah 28:16–17: 'See, I lay a stone in Zion, a tested stone, a precious cornerstone for a sure foundation; the one who trusts will never be dismayed. I will make justice the measuring line and righteousness the plumb-line; hail will sweep away your refuge, the lie, and water will overflow your hiding-place.' Powerful!

3. Jesus' strategy in telling some parables may have been less straight teaching than to paint pictures which teased people to wonder and to ask questions.

4. It's sometimes hard for us to appreciate just how subversive Jesus was!

Week 3: Parables told to friends and disciples

Opening Icebreaker and Worship

Again, encourage people to keep their stories in the Icebreaker brief and to the point. Understanding some of this week's parables isn't easy. We need the Holy Spirit to lead us into all truth – which is reached not only through the intellect but through our spirits aligning themselves in relationship with Him. The best way I know of to do that is through worship, where, as we give our love to Him, He affirms His love for us and shows us more of Himself. One good way into worship is to thank Him for specific things.

If you can find the poem 'The Bright Field' by R.S. Thomas – either in a book, perhaps from a library, or a search engine on the Internet – try reading it out loud to inspire your worship. Imagine standing looking at the view from a Welsh hillside. Clouds passing across the sun allow just one field to be lit. I love the way the poet takes Jesus' parable and imagines himself further, into an everyday worshipful life which hums with the difference which God makes.

Aim of the Session

To help one another see more in Jesus and turn that depth of seeing into practice, particularly in terms of communicating truths about Him to our friends.

Discussion Starters

1. Luke 16:1–15. Several commentators say that the rich man would have been charging interest, contrary to Jewish precept – and that the manager has shrewdly reduced the debtors' bills by the amount of that interest, pushing his master off the moral high ground.

2. Luke chapter 18 begins with the word 'Then'. Glance back and you'll find the disciples had been asking when the kingdom of God would come. The kingdom of God is another way of saying 'God's rule and reign of justice and mercy on this earth' – and those who 'cry out to him' even though things are desperate now, will get justice.

3. In the parable of the weeds it's helpful to know that enemies really were known to sow weed seeds in people's crops – and that darnel, the weed in question, looks very similar to wheat after germination. Its roots entwine around those of the wheat, so weeding out the darnel would destroy both crops. There's great hope in this parable for those who worry about the way evil people prosper alongside the good.

4. A pearl was considered the most precious and beautiful of things, but a huge net would have hauled in everything between two boats – the 'clean' and the 'unclean'. A bit of a shock here, then! If questions come up about hell, gnashing of teeth etcetera, it might be helpful to look at Revelation 20:11–15.

I always felt sorry for the man with the one talent until someone pointed out that his irredeemable mistake wasn't self-doubt. Rather, his belief that his master (God) was 'hard' meant the man couldn't access His grace to do His work.

5. In the Near East of Jesus' day, sheep and goats looked very similar and often grazed together. They needed

separating at night because, according to Ruth Etchells (*op. cit.*), sheep need air and goats shelter. She goes on to point out how Jesus was naked, imprisoned, thirsty etcetera on the cross – and that we're judged by our response to Him there.

John's Gospel records a slightly different kind of parable Jesus told His disciples. You might like to look at, for example, 12:24 (the seed falling to the ground and dying); the acted parable of washing feet in 13:1–17; extended imagery of vine and branches in 15:1–8.

Week 4: Parables told to enemies

Opening Icebreaker and Worship
In the Icebreaker think of ordinary life not God-talk here. For your worship you could also listen to a hymn on CD or tape. Maybe Rembrandt's famous picture of *The Return of the Prodigal Son* would help focus your understanding and worship. You should be able to find it in a library book or by doing a picture search on the Internet. For some spiritual illumination on it, read Henri Nouwen's book, *The Return of the Prodigal Son* (DLT, 1994).

Aim of the Session
- To see more clearly how Jesus' perspective differs from that of His enemies so that we can align ourselves with Jesus rather than with religion.
- To learn how to communicate with those who hold rigid positions which differ greatly from God's.
- To learn something about conflict – and true and false authority.

These are all areas where Christians have not done too well over the years – think of the Crusades, the Inquisition; think of conflicts such as Northern Ireland. All provide evidence for those who say 'faith is dangerous

– avoid it!' And it is true that faith without love, without the ability to imagine yourself in someone else's shoes, is highly dangerous. It's also been dangerous for those who did exercise faith with love and imagination. Many paid the price, like Jesus, by dying for their faith. If you come to talk about these things, remind the group that there have been vast numbers of 'ordinary' unsung Christians who love Jesus and give everything to include others in His kingdom of love.

Discussion Starters

1. Ten silver coins were hardly a fortune. The woman must have been very poor – and the party she gave sounds lavish, out of all proportion to the finding.

2. The story of the rich man and Lazarus, though told to the disciples, was probably overheard by the religious Jews or occasioned by questions the disciples asked about their attitude. W.E.O. Oesterley, in *The Gospel Parables in the Light of their Jewish Background*, makes the point about repenting in Hades and also quotes rabbinical examples similar to, yet very different from, this parable. Parables are not the place to look for detailed doctrine so don't get involved in making conclusions about the nature of heaven and hell from this story. It's interesting, though, that the rich man persists in thinking of Lazarus as his servant, even when the poor man is in glory and the rich one in shame and torment.

3. I've met just a few Christian leaders who combine real humility with real authority. They remind me so much of Jesus.

4. My church homegroup welcomes four extra people once a month who range from atheists to agnostics. They ask questions, some of which have a weight of anger or hurt behind them. We've often found it helpful to turn someone's question around and ask, 'What do you think?'

It's surprising how often they see the answer to their own questions! On other occasions we've told stories, given analogies or unexpected answers (they've thought Christians believed the oddest things!). It's been exciting to watch many of their difficulties disappear – and we're privileged that they are prepared to be so honest. Can your group be as honest in responding to the confrontational questions Jesus is asking of them in this passage?

Week 5: Parables told to individuals who asked questions

Opening Icebreaker and Worship

This session requires a large degree of honesty and maybe a willingness to change our thinking and behaviour. It may show up some people's sense of inadequacy. Watch out that sensitive and honest types are not hurt by other Christians in the group. The 'sword of the Spirit, which is the word of truth' is not for sticking down throats! Remind people that there is no condemnation for those who love God. When He convicts us that change is necessary, He shows us the way and gives us the means.

Questions in the Psalms: for example 6 or 10, 79 or 80. If you read on, normally God gives an answer, or His felt presence changes everything. With Psalm 88, the darkest of all, there are no answers, no presence, yet this psalm appears in the Jewish 'hymn book' for use in their worship.

Aims of the Session

• To provoke questions about the inclusivity of God's kingdom. I suspect most of us are less inclusive than He is, so this may provoke consternation, which is often a cloak for prejudice. Be prayerful, be wise. If feelings run high, stop the discussion, come before the cross and let the peace of the Holy Spirit be the arbiter.

• To consider how our lives could provoke faith-questions from the individuals we know outside the Church.

'When your children ask you … say …' examples are Exodus 12:26–27 and Joshua 4:6–7.

Further examples of Jesus answering individuals' questions with often extended comparison-parables are, Nicodemus in John 3, the Samaritan woman in John 4, Martha in John 11:25–26 and Peter in John 21. Luke 12:13–21; 13:3–30; 14:15–24; 18:18–25 are all statements or questions asked by individuals which we look at in other sessions. Mark 2:15–22 also appears in Luke 5:27–35 and Matthew 9:14–17.

Discussion Starters
1. John's disciples ask the same questions in Matthew. Be aware that behaviour speaks louder than words. There was once a Town Hall where a number of Christians' quiet witness over the years was largely undone when a new man arrived to head up a department. Within a week he'd managed to annoy everyone in the building. He made some very bad decisions, then announced they all ought to become more like he was – a Christian. Remind people too that, before they commit to Jesus, most people need several encounters with different Christians who each point them in some way towards Him.

2. You might like to think of some present-day examples of people who love Jesus the most because they have been forgiven most.

3. Do read the whole of the story in Chronicles beforehand, if you have time.

Do you know the joke about the newcomer being shown round heaven? He saw various groups of people worshipping God in their different ways, then was led right away from the others to the top of a hill, where he could hear yet more sounds of worship coming from behind a fence. His guide urged 'Shhh!' as the newcomer peered through a knot-hole in the fence. They tiptoed back down the hill. 'What was that all about?' the new citizen asked. 'Ah – you see, that group think no one else is here.'

4. Christians, especially women, are prone to unhelpful comparisons: 'I'm not as good as she is, and never will be!' Steer the group towards positive responses – for example someone's generosity inspiring their own – or positive repentance, for example a person might recall the story of the Emperor's new clothes and turn away from some foolishness.

Don't seek intellectual or 'theological' explanations of grace – think example and story!

Week 6: Parables told to the rich and powerful, or the nation

Opening Icebreaker and Worship
The person should be someone alive today and not someone in the Bible, not Jesus. The discussion may touch on different kinds of importance, wealth and influence.

Aims of the Session
• To see Jesus' directness in the face of those who seemed to be powerful or wealthy.
• To learn from Him about how we might communicate Him to them.
• And about how we might live rightly in His eternal kingdom.
This week involves high challenge! People may well be convicted and need to repent – to change their thinking, attitudes, even direction. If God speaks to any about

repentance or change, make sure they don't leave feeling condemned, useless or 'stuck'. God always shines a lamp for our feet when He wants us to walk forwards!

Most of us live in a multi-faith society – where the 'faiths' include intellectual atheism, as well as *acting* as though God doesn't exist. Jesus, in most of these passages, is talking to people following the Jewish religion and could appeal to Scripture when addressing them. Our yelling 'But the Bible says …' is often counter-productive today because so many don't recognise its authority. Remind people in your group, if they come up with that 'excuse', that the Early Church grew in a multi-faith context.

Sometimes I think that the messages and activities of churches appear irrelevant to most outsiders. Outside the Church people are always discussing questions of wealth, power and authority, but churches don't often address these issues, not in ways outsiders understand, anyway. But these important questions are linked with religion as well as with politics, sociology and economics. I believe Christians have something to say about 'who is in control' – if only we can find effective ways of saying it! And, more importantly, of living it.

Someone who uses authority and/or money with real humility demonstrates that life, real life, isn't about wealth, power or fame, but about something much better, something eternal, something emanating from an unconditional, *agapé* love which could only come from God and which makes a real difference to our world. Jesus Himself certainly wasn't powerful, rich or important within His nation – yet some people then, and many since, have recognised the authority God gave Him. Besides His own Son, God has also given authority to many 'ordinary' people over the years, from Old Testament prophets to Martin Luther King. You might want to spend some time praying for Him to raise up such people in your nation

– as well as asking Him to work through you, within whatever spheres of influence you have.

Discussion Starters

4. Many Jews did follow Jesus – while many churches haven't, over the centuries. I wonder how many 'bad news' stories might have been averted had all professing Christians really followed Jesus and lived as He intended?

5. Not all Pharisees were hardened against Jesus. Consider Nicodemus, for example.

Week 7: 'I will open my mouth in parables'

Opening Icebreaker and Worship

Limit it to a few sermon illustrations or you could be there all night!

If you're not used to this kind of worship, and to give people confidence and safe boundaries, read 1 Corinthians 14:26 which says: 'When you come together, everyone has a hymn, or a word of instruction, a revelation, a tongue or an interpretation. All of these must be done for the strengthening of the church'; and/or Colossians 3:16: 'Let the word of Christ dwell in you richly as you teach and admonish one another with all wisdom, and as you sing psalms, hymns and spiritual songs with gratitude in your hearts to God.'

Aim of the Session

'Go forth and tell' – plus some summing up.

Discussion Starters

1. It might be good if you, as leader, have read the whole of Psalm 78. Salvation history isn't restricted to people's 'conversion experience'.
2. Information about fig trees which you may find useful:

highly productive – fruits ten months of the year, so was planted in most fields and vineyards; fruits three years after planting: first year's fruit given to God; no flowers visible but hundreds exist inside the fruit. Still, after researching and reading the commentaries, I don't fully understand Jesus' words and actions concerning figs. To me the most useful pointer is that the cursing of the fig tree, in Mark's Gospel, comes within the context of the cleansing of the Temple, as almost a visible parable of it.

I am just about old enough to remember Peter Cook and Dudley Moore having one of their philosophical 'Pete 'n Dud' conversations. 'Revd. So-and-so' had told one of them that all those people in far-off lands who have never heard of Jesus won't go to hell, while anyone who has heard and rejected Him will. The pair came to the entirely logical conclusion that it was a real sin to tell ignorant people about Jesus.

I wonder if that's why some of Jesus' parables are hard to understand? I've heard, this very week, of a Christian who tells almost complete strangers riddles and then wanders off. It seems they seek him out later and start talking about God. And my physiotherapist (mentioned earlier) turns out to be a Christian – which explains why I had the impression he was praying for me before he started treatment. He prays for all his patients – and he pointed out three abstract/symbolist pictures on the walls that often spark God-conversations. Painted by a friend of his when on his own journey to Christ, their meaning takes some teasing out. I wasn't too clear about it even after an explanation. 'Before I met Jesus a few years ago, I hated it if anyone confronted me head-on with the gospel,' said the physio, 'but these intrigue people.' Better first to intrigue someone, than to face them with a point blank decision to accept or reject Jesus. There are lived, spoken, prayed and felt parables of God's kingdom all over that treatment room.

3. Gospel truth isn't much good unless it's lived. Jesus' parables parallel His life and actions.

If it's not easy to tell parables about God and His kingdom, it's certainly not easy to be one! This week's study reviews some of what you've discussed earlier. Try to spend some time praying with one another about what you've learned and about how you are applying it to your lives. Encourage one another. Don't stop after this session. Support and pray for each other when the going gets tough and keep telling each other stories of what God is doing in and through one another.

NATIONAL DISTRIBUTORS

UK: (and countries not listed below)
CWR, Waverley Abbey House, Waverley Lane, Farnham, Surrey GU9 8EP.
Tel: (01252) 784700 Outside UK (44) 1252 784700 Email: mail@cwr.org.uk

AUSTRALIA: KI Entertainment, Unit 21 317-321 Woodpark Road, Smithfield, New South
Wales 2164 Tel: 1 800 850 777 Fax: 02 9604 3699 Email: sales@kientertainment.com.au

CANADA: David C Cook Distribution Canada, PO Box 98, 55 Woodslee Avenue, Paris,
Ontario N3L 3E5 Tel: 1800 263 2664 Email: joy.kearley@davidccook.ca

GHANA: Challenge Enterprises of Ghana, PO Box 5723, Accra Tel: (021) 222437/223249
Fax: (021) 226227 Email: ceg@africaonline.com.gh

HONG KONG: Cross Communications Ltd, 11/F Ko's House, 577 Nathan Road, Kowloon
Tel: 2780 1188 Fax: 2770 6229 Email: cross@crosshk.com

INDIA: Crystal Communications, Plot No. 125, Road No. 7, T.M.C, Mahendra Hills, East
Marredpally, Secunderabad - 500026 Tel/Fax: (040) 27737145
Email: crystal_edwj@rediffmail.com

KENYA: Keswick Books and Gifts Ltd, PO Box 10242-00400, Nairobi
Tel: (020) 2226047/312639 Email: sales.keswick@africaonline.co.ke

MALAYSIA: Canaanland Distributors Sdn Bhd, No. 25 Jalan PJU 1A/41B, NZX
Commercial Centre, Ara Jaya, 47301 Petaling Jaya, Selangor
Tel: (03) 7885 0540/1/2 Fax: (03) 7885 0545 Email: info@canaanland.com.my

Salvation Publishing & Distribution Sdn Bhd, 23 Jalan SS 2/64, 47300 Petaling Jaya,
Selangor Tel: (03) 78766411/78766797 Fax: (03) 78757066/78756360
Email: info@salvationbookcentre.com

NEW ZEALAND: KI Entertainment, Unit 21 317-321 Woodpark Road, Smithfield, New
South Wales 2164, Australia Tel: 0 800 850 777 Fax: +612 9604 3699
Email: sales@kientertainment.com.au

NIGERIA: FBFM, Helen Baugh House, 96 St Finbarr's College Road, Akoka, Lagos
Tel: (+234) 01-7747429, 08075201777, 08186337699, 08154453905
Email: fbfm_1@yahoo.com

PHILIPPINES: OMF Literature Inc, 776 Boni Avenue, Mandaluyong City
Tel: (02) 531 2183 Fax: (02) 531 1960 Email: gloadlaon@omflit.com

SINGAPORE: Alby Commercial Enterprises Pte Ltd, 95 Kallang Avenue #04-00, AIS
Industrial Building, 339420 Tel: (+65) 629 27238 Fax: (+65) 629 27235
Email: marketing@alby.com.sg

SOUTH AFRICA: Life Media & Distribution, Unit 20, Tungesten Industrial Park, 7 C R
Swart Drive, Strydompark 2125 Tel: (+27) 0117924277 Fax: (+27) 0117924512
Email: orders@lifemedia.co.za

SRI LANKA: Christombu Publications (Pvt) Ltd, Bartleet House, 65 Braybrooke Place,
Colombo 2 Tel: (+941) 2421073/2447665 Email: christombupublications@gmail.com

USA: David C Cook Distribution Canada, PO Box 98, 55 Woodslee Avenue, Paris,
Ontario N3L 3E5, Canada Tel: 1800 263 2664 Email: joy.kearley@davidccook.ca

CWR is a Registered Charity - Number 294387
CWR is a Limited Company registered in England - Registration Number 1990308

Seminars and events

Waverley Abbey College

Publishing and media

Conference facilities

Transforming lives

CWR's vision is to enable people to experience personal transformation through applying God's Word to their lives and relationships.

Our Bible-based training and resources help people around the world to:

• Grow in their walk with God
• Understand and apply Scripture to their lives
• Resource themselves and their church
• Develop pastoral care and counselling skills
• Train for leadership
• Strengthen relationships, marriage and family life and much more.

Our insightful writers provide daily Bible-reading notes and other resources for all ages, and our experienced course designers and presenters have gained an international reputation for excellence and effectiveness.

CWR's Training and Conference Centres in Surrey and East Sussex, England, provide excellent facilities in idyllic settings – ideal for both learning and spiritual refreshment.

CWR Applying God's Word
to everyday life and relationships

CWR, Waverley Abbey House,
Waverley Lane, Farnham,
Surrey GU9 8EP, UK

Telephone: **+44 (0)1252 784700**
Email: **info@cwr.org.uk**
Website: **www.cwr.org.uk**

Registered Charity No. 294387
Company Registration No. 1990308

Latest resource

Abraham - Adventures of Faith
by Dave Edwins

Abraham's example of faith in tough times can help us grow in obedience, prayer and resolve during our own times of testing. Follow in the footsteps of the original adventurer in faith.

ISBN: 978-1-78259-089-7

Luke - A Prescription for Living
by John Houghton

How should we live in today's world? Luke records in his Gospel a detailed historical account of Jesus and shows us how Jesus provides a prescription for living in today's world, and for the future.

ISBN: 978-1-78259-270-9

The bestselling *Cover to Cover* Bible Study Series

1 Corinthians
Growing a Spirit-filled church
ISBN: 978-1-85345-374-8

2 Corinthians
Restoring harmony
ISBN: 978-1-85345-551-3

1 Peter
Good reasons for hope
ISBN: 978-1-78259-088-0

1 Timothy
Healthy churches –
effective Christians
ISBN: 978-1-85345-291-8

23rd Psalm
The Lord is my shepherd
ISBN: 978-1-85345-449-3

2 Timothy and Titus
Vital Christianity
ISBN: 978-1-85345-338-0

Abraham
Adventures of faith
ISBN: 978-1-78259-089-7

Acts 1–12
Church on the move
ISBN: 978-1-85345-574-2

Acts 13–28
To the ends of the earth
ISBN: 978-1-85345-592-6

Barnabas
Son of encouragement
ISBN: 978-1-85345-911-5

Bible Genres
Hearing what the Bible really says
ISBN: 978-1-85345-987-0

Daniel
Living boldly for God
ISBN: 978-1-85345-986-3

Ecclesiastes
Hard questions and
spiritual answers
ISBN: 978-1-85345-371-7

Elijah
A man and his God
ISBN: 978-1-85345-575-9

Ephesians
Claiming your inheritance
ISBN: 978-1-85345-229-1

Esther
For such a time as this
ISBN: 978-1-85345-511-7

Fruit of the Spirit
Growing more like Jesus
ISBN: 978-1-85345-375-5

Galatians
Freedom in Christ
ISBN: 978-1-85345-648-0

Genesis 1–11
Foundations of reality
ISBN: 978-1-85345-404-2

God's Rescue Plan
Finding God's fingerprints
on human history
ISBN: 978-1-85345-294-9

Great Prayers of the Bible
Applying them to our lives today
ISBN: 978-1-85345-253-6

Hebrews
Jesus – simply the best
ISBN: 978-1-85345-337-3

Hosea
The love that never fails
ISBN: 978-1-85345-290-1

Isaiah 1–39
Prophet to the nations
ISBN: 978-1-85345-510-0

Isaiah 40–66
Prophet of restoration
ISBN: 978-1-85345-550-6

James
Faith in action
ISBN: 978-1-85345-293-2

Jeremiah
The passionate prophet
ISBN: 978-1-85345-372-4

John's Gospel
Exploring the seven miraculous signs
ISBN: 978-1-85345-295-6

Joseph
The power of forgiveness and reconciliation
ISBN: 978-1-85345-252-9

Judges 1–8
The spiral of faith
ISBN: 978-1-85345-681-7

Judges 9–21
Learning to live God's way
ISBN: 978-1-85345-910-8

Luke
A prescription for living
ISBN: 978-1-78259-270-9

Mark
Life as it is meant to be lived
ISBN: 978-1-85345-233-8

Moses
Face to face with God
ISBN: 978-1-85345-336-6

Names of God
Exploring the depths of God's character
ISBN: 978-1-85345-680-0

Nehemiah
Principles for life
ISBN: 978-1-85345-335-9

Parables
Communicating God on earth
ISBN: 978-1-85345-340-3

Philemon
From slavery to freedom
ISBN: 978-1-85345-453-0

Philippians
Living for the sake of the gospel
ISBN: 978-1-85345-421-9

Prayers of Jesus
Hearing His heartbeat
ISBN: 978-1-85345-647-3

Proverbs
Living a life of wisdom
ISBN: 978-1-85345-373-1

Revelation 1–3
Christ's call to the Church
ISBN: 978-1-85345-461-5

Revelation 4–22
The Lamb wins! Christ's final victory
ISBN: 978-1-85345-411-0

Rivers of Justice
Responding to God's call to righteousness today
ISBN: 978-1-85345-339-7

Ruth
Loving kindness in action
ISBN: 978-1-85345-231-4

The Covenants
God's promises and their relevance today
ISBN: 978-1-85345-255-0

The Creed
Belief in action
ISBN: 978-1-78259-202-0

The Divine Blueprint
God's extraordinary power in ordinary lives
ISBN: 978-1-85345-292-5

The Holy Spirit
Understanding and experiencing Him
ISBN: 978-1-85345-254-3

The Image of God
His attributes and character
ISBN: 978-1-85345-228-4

The Kingdom
Studies from Matthew's Gospel
ISBN: 978-1-85345-251-2

The Letter to the Colossians
In Christ alone
ISBN: 978-1-85345-405-9

The Letter to the Romans
Good news for everyone
ISBN: 978-1-85345-250-5

The Lord's Prayer
Praying Jesus' way
ISBN: 978-1-85345-460-8

The Prodigal Son
Amazing grace
ISBN: 978-1-85345-412-7

The Second Coming
Living in the light of Jesus' return
ISBN: 978-1-85345-422-6

The Sermon on the Mount
Life within the new covenant
ISBN: 978-1-85345-370-0

The Tabernacle
Entering into God's presence
ISBN: 978-1-85345-230-7

The Ten Commandments
Living God's Way
ISBN: 978-1-85345-593-3

The Uniqueness of our Faith
What makes Christianity distinctive?
ISBN: 978-1-85345-232-1

For current prices or to order visit www.cwr.org.uk/store
Available online or from Christian bookshops.

Continue transforming your daily walk with God.

Every Day with Jesus

With around half a million readers, this insightful devotional by Selwyn Hughes is one of the most popular daily Bible reading tools in the world. A large-print edition is also available.
72-page booklets, 120x170mm

Life Every Day

Apply the Bible to life each day with these challenging life-application notes written by international speaker and well-known author Jeff Lucas.
64-page booklets, 120x170mm

Inspiring Women Every Day

Written by women for women of all ages and from all walks of life. These notes will help to build faith and bring encouragement and inspiration to the lives and hearts of Christian women.
64-page booklets, 120x170mm

Cover to Cover Every Day

Study one Old Testament and one New Testament book in depth with each issue, and a psalm every weekend. Covers every book of the Bible in five years.
64-page booklets, 120x170mm

For current price or to order visit www.cwr.org.uk/store
Available online or from Christian bookshops.

Journey through the Bible as it happened – in a year of daily readings

Read through the entire Bible in a year with 366 daily readings from the New International Version (NIV) arranged in chronological order.

Beautiful charts, maps, illustrations and diagrams make the biblical background vivid, timelines enable you to track your progress, and a daily commentary helps you to apply what you read to your life.

A special website also provides character studies, insightful articles, photos of archaeological sites and much more for increased understanding and insight.

Cover to Cover Complete – NIV Edition
1600 pages, hardback with ribbon marker, 140x215mm
ISBN: 978-1-85345-804-0

smallGroup central

All of our small group ideas and resources in one place

Online:

www.smallgroupcentral.org.uk
is an exciting new website filled with
free video teaching, free tools and a
whole host of ideas.

On the road:

We provide a range of seminars
themed for small groups. If you
would like us to bring a seminar to
your local community, contacts us at
hello@smallgroupcentral.org.uk

In print:

Books, study guides and DVDs
covering an extensive list of themes,
Bible books and life issues.

Log on and find out more at:
www.smallgroupcentral.org.uk